Numbers and Shapes

Just for Kids

Dr. LaKeisha Jeanne Cole

To order additional copies of this book, contact:
Xlibris
1-888-795-4274
www.Xlibris.com
Orders@Xlibris.com

ISBN: Softcover   978-1-7960-7704-9
       EBook   978-1-7960-7703-2

Print information available on the last page

Rev. date: 12/09/2019

one big blue rectangle

1

two big red octagons

2 8 2

three oval shapes

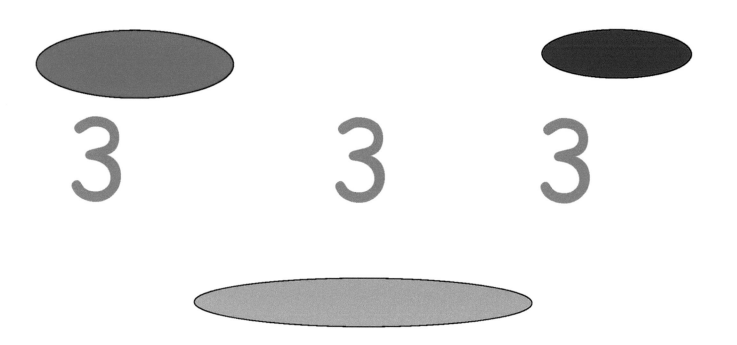

four green diamonds

five triangles

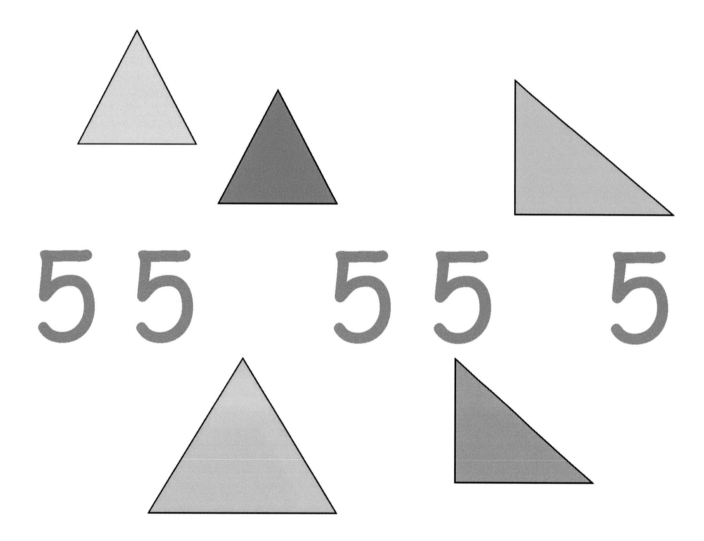

six flat purple ovals

seven flat pink squares

eight great shapes

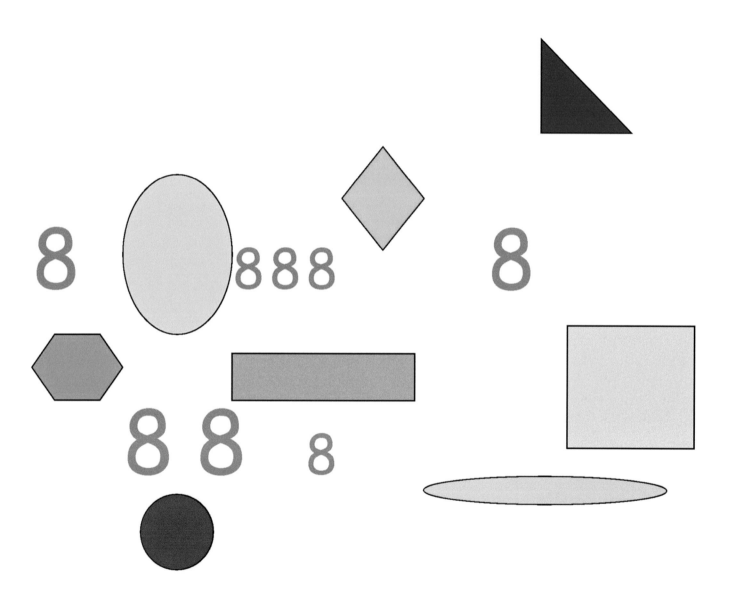

nine colorful circles

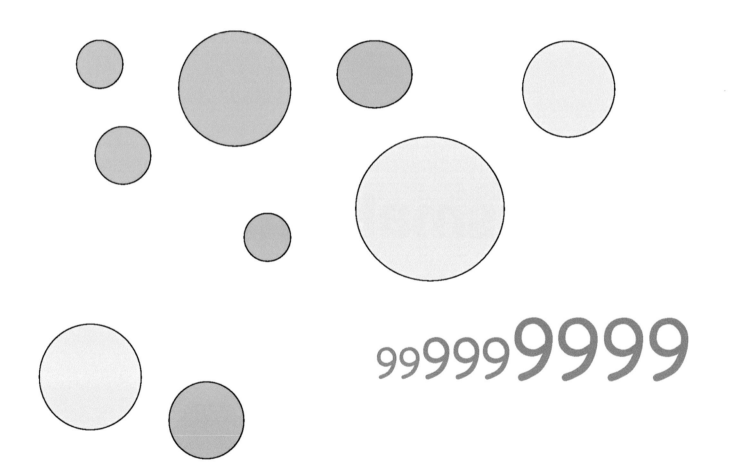

999999999

ten small shapes

Printed in the United States
By Bookmasters